Tales of Jesus

Tales of Jesus

TREASURE PRESS

First published in Great Britain in 1982 by
Cathay Books Limited

This edition published in 1986 by
Treasure Press
59 Grosvenor Street
London W1

ISBN 1 85051 107 1

Printed in Hong Kong

The first Christmas	6
The boy Jesus is missing	8
Jesus in the wilderness	10
The Disciples of Jesus	12
A miracle at a wedding	14
Healing the sick	16
Jesus and the Sabbath Day	18
The pool at Bethesda	20
A woman's tears	22
The stories Jesus told	24
The workers in the vineyard	26
Feeding the multitude	28
Jesus walks on the water	30
The madman	32
A little girl is given life	34
A shining light	36
Jesus and the rich man	38
The good Samaritan	40
The Prodigal Son	42
The Tax Collector	44
The raising of Lazarus	46
The man born blind	48
The man who was deaf	50
The ten lepers	52
The woman at the well	54
Palm Sunday	56
Jesus is betrayed	58
The stranger on the road	60
More parables of Jesus	62
Two houses	64

The first Christmas

Once upon a time, nearly two thousand years ago, there was a certain carpenter, who was called Joseph. He lived in the little village of Nazareth, which is in the area known today as the Holy Land. His gentle and dearly loved wife, Mary, was expecting a baby. This was a very special baby, for an angel had come to Joseph and told him that when the child was born it was to be called Jesus, which means 'Saviour.' 'For he shall save people from their sins,' the angel had explained.

In those days the country was ruled by the far-off city of Rome, then a mighty power in the world. One day, the people of Nazareth learned that their Roman ruler had a new order for them. It was announced that everyone who had left the place where they had been born had to return at once, so that their names could be entered in a register. Joseph and Mary sighed. This meant that they would have to travel all the way from Nazareth to Bethlehem, many miles away.

Joseph and Mary arrived at last in Bethlehem, but they found the place crowded with many other people who had come to register. The inns were all full and the only place they could find to spend the night was a stable. They even had to share this with some cattle.

It was in this cold and miserable stable that the baby Jesus was born.

Not very far away, some shepherds were huddled together, guarding their sheep, for hungry wolves were on the prowl. Suddenly an angel appeared in a dazzling shimmering light and spoke to them.

'Fear not,' he said, as the shepherds shrank before his awesome splendour. 'Fear not for I bring you joyful news. This night in Bethlehem, is born a saviour for all mankind. He is Christ the Lord. You will find him lying in a manger in a stable.'

Then the angel disappeared.

Gathering their scattered wits together, the shepherds hurried to the stable. There, they found the child, and fell to their knees in worship.

High above the lowly stable, a new star, more brilliant and bigger than any other, appeared in the heavens shining brightly.

Far, far away to the East, three wise men saw this star and guessed that it signalled the birth of a great new king.

The three wise men decided to seek him out and give him presents to honour his birth. Without delay they set out, using the new star as their guide. Coming at last to the capital city of Jerusalem, they made their way to the palace of the King, expecting to find the royal baby there.

The King, whose name was Herod, at first welcomed the wise men. But he was puzzled and angry when they insisted that they were searching for a new-born king. There had been no recent births in his family.

Cunningly, he asked the wise men to tell him all they knew about the new king. Then he said: 'Go forth and find this child. Then return here and tell me where he is so that I, too, might go and worship him.'

But he added to himself 'And when I know where this child is, he shall die, for there shall be no other king than me.'

Once again, the three wise men set out, still following the bright star. Finally it led them to the village of Bethlehem where they found the baby Jesus with his mother and father. Kneeling before the child, they worshipped him. Then, they presented their gifts of gold, frankincense and myrrh, which were very precious in the days when Jesus was born.

The next day, the three wise men set out for home. They did not return by way of Jerusalem, because God had warned them in a dream that Herod planned to kill little Jesus.

Months passed. When Herod realized that the three wise men were not returning with news of the new king's birthplace, he flew into a terrible rage. He ordered that every child aged two and under, living in Bethlehem and the surrounding countryside, should be put to death.

Herod's soldiers did not find Jesus in their search for children, because Mary and Joseph had already fled with him to Egypt. One night, while Joseph was sleeping, an angel had appeared to him and warned him to leave

Bethlehem at once, taking his family.

Joseph, Mary and Jesus settled in Egypt and remained there until the evil King Herod died. Then Joseph took his wife and child to Nazareth, the village that he and Mary had left so many years before. Here Jesus grew up, helping his father with his carpentry, until he was twelve years old. That year, his parents took him to Jerusalem for the Feast of the Passover.

It was to prove a most surprising journey for the parents of Jesus.

The boy Jesus is missing

On reaching the age of thirteen, each Jewish boy is regarded as a man and becomes subject to the law and all its regulations. Jesus was twelve years old when his parents, Mary and Joseph, decided it was time he went with them to Jerusalem where, each year, they celebrated the Feast of the Passover.

Long, long before Jesus was born, his forefathers, the Israelites, had been slaves in the land of Egypt. Moses, their leader, had striven to free his people from the Pharaoh, the ruler of Egypt. Pharaoh had always refused Moses' request.

At last, Moses brought down on the heads of the Egyptians six terrible plagues. During each one, the Pharaoh started to think that it might be a good idea to release the Israelites. Then, as each plague ended, he hardened his heart and swore that his Jewish slaves should never be freed.

Then came the seventh and last punishing blow, for God had decided to take a hand himself in freeing the Israelites. In the course of one dreadful night, he passed over the land of Egypt. All the first-born in the country died – the first-born of every animal and every human except the Jews', even Pharaoh's eldest and much-beloved son.

This was all too much for that ruthless Pharaoh. He allowed the Israelites to leave Egypt. From that time onwards, the Jews have held a feast, once a year, to commemorate the night when God 'passed over' the families of the Israelites, and took his terrible toll of the Egyptians.

So Joseph set off, leading an ass, on whose sturdy back was seated the gentle Mary. Alongside stumbled the twelve-year-old Jesus. Doubtless they would have joined many other pilgrims toiling along the rocky ways and through the dusty highways towards the distant city of Jerusalem.

There for the first time Jesus saw the great temple, the busy streets and crowds of people

pouring in to celebrate the Passover. According to Jewish law, all adult males had to attend this feast.

The Feast of the Passover lasted a full week but those attending did not have to stay for more than two days. With such a long journey home, Joseph and Mary probably left after two days, together with several friends.

Throughout the first day of their journey home, Mary and Joseph did not actually see Jesus, for there were many people in the party. They probably thought that the lad was with the other boys in the group.

As dusk fell, Joseph and Mary suddenly

discovered that Jesus was not with them. As time went by and he failed to appear, they became anxious and went around the family groups asking if anyone had seen him. No one had. The boy Jesus was missing!

'He must still be celebrating in Jerusalem,' decided Joseph. 'We must return there first thing in the morning and look for him.'

Back in Jerusalem, Mary and Joseph spent three days searching for Jesus everywhere. Tired and worried they finally went into the temple. To their astonishment there he was, seated among the teachers and doctors of law.

It was most unusual to see a mere boy of twelve deep in conversation with men four and five times his age. He was asking them many questions which they found amazing, and he answered their questions with an understanding unheard of in someone so young.

Mary was near to tears with relief at finding her son but also angry that he had not told either of his parents where he was.

'Why have you caused us so much worry?' she asked. 'We have been looking for you everywhere.'

'But surely,' Jesus replied, 'you should have known I would be in my Father's house.' Jesus was reminding Mary that he was God's son.

Jesus in the wilderness

Out of the wilderness of Judah came a most unusual figure. He was a man with fiery eyes, long straggling hair and beard, dressed in a ragged jerkin made of camel's hair.

His name was John, a preacher and a deeply religious man. He never drank wine, only water, and he ate the kind of food that was only eaten by the very poor – wild honey and locusts boiled in salt water and dried.

John was a relation of Jesus, for he was the son of Mary's cousin, He was always warning people that they should repent of their sins and henceforth do good deeds as proof of their true repentance.

Hundreds of people listened and believed all that John was preaching. They streamed towards the River Jordan where John was waiting for them. There, up to his waist in water, he baptized all those people who came to him and swore to lead new lives. For this reason, John became known as 'John the Baptist'.

Jesus was now a man of thirty years, still living with his mother. His father Joseph was by now dead. When Jesus was told of John the Baptist's activities, it seemed to him a call from God. Bidding his mother farewell, he set out for the River Jordan and joined the queue of people awaiting baptism.

Instantly, John pointed to Jesus. 'Behold the Lamb of God,' he shouted. 'He who beareth away the sin of the world.'

He motioned to Jesus to come forward. 'I should not be baptizing you,' he said in a quieter voice. '*You* should be baptizing me.'

To this Jesus replied, 'You must baptize me for only in this way can we do the righteous will of God.'

John obediently baptized Jesus. As Jesus turned to make his way back to the river bank, it seemed to John that a beautiful white dove rested on his cousin's shoulder. Then came a voice from heaven saying 'This is my well-beloved son, in whom I am well pleased.'

John's soul must have been filled with wonder as he watched Jesus walk away.

It is from this moment that the teaching, or ministry, of Jesus begins. He had only three more years of life left to him.

Jesus now went into the wilderness so that he could be alone to pray to God his Father in heaven. He remained out in that desolate country for forty days and nights, without food and with only wild beasts for company.

Towards the end, a harsh wind arose and beat hot sand into the tired body of Jesus. He was now faint with thirst and starvation. In

the wind Jesus heard the sinister voice of Satan the devil, tempting him by saying, 'If you really are the Son of God you can turn these stones into bread and eat them.'

Although so weak and desperately hungry, Jesus recognized Satan's cunning and replied, 'Man does not live by bread alone but by every word of God.' Had Jesus done as the devil suggested, He would have been using his great power purely for selfish reasons.

Next, taking advantage of Jesus's exhausted state, the devil caused him to imagine he was standing on the roof of the great temple in Jerusalem, and said, 'If you are the Son of God, throw yourself down, for it is written that the angels of God will bear you up before you hit the ground.'

But Jesus knew that no one should test God by stupidly taking risks and then asking the Lord to perform unnecessary miracles. So he replied to Satan, 'It is also written, "Thou shalt not tempt the Lord thy God." '

Still not put off, the devil tried once more. This time he made Jesus believe he was standing on top of the highest mountain in the whole world. He said in a sly and tempting way, 'Here below you are all the kingdoms of the world and all the power they command. All this will I give you if you will first fall down and worship me.'

Jesus knew that to agree to this would mean that he would be ruled by Satan, and people on earth would be condemned to a life of misery and sin. So he replied 'Away with you, Satan, for it is written, "You must worship the Lord your God and him only must you serve." '

Beaten, the devil slunk away for there was nothing more with which he could tempt Jesus.

Angels of the Lord now came to take care of Jesus for he was utterly exhausted after his battle of wits with the devil.

The Disciples of Jesus

Leaving the wilderness behind him, Jesus returned to Nazareth and began to teach. He knew that he had come to earth to set up God's Kingdom – a kingdom in which there would be no evil, but only love, peace and joy. It was a mighty task indeed, difficult even for the Son of God, and Jesus had so little time in which to do it.

Jesus needed the help of other people, good devout men who would accompany him on his long journeys and share his hardships. But first he went to find John the Baptist once again, for a meeting that was to prove their last.

Jesus found John, calling upon his listeners to repent. Around him stood several of his followers, or disciples. When John saw Jesus he cried out, 'Behold the Lamb of God who bears away the sin of the world.' Jesus smiled, spoke a few words of farewell to John and strode away.

Some time later, Jesus was walking along the shore of the Sea of Galilee, near the village of Capernaum. He saw two fishermen casting their nets into the sea. They were brothers, by name Andrew and Simon Peter, who liked to be known simply as Peter. Jesus recognized them. Had they not been two of the disciples of John the Baptist, who had stood beside that strange preacher when last Jesus had seen him?

There was something about these two good men that touched the heart of Jesus. As their boat neared the shore, Jesus spoke to them. 'Follow me and I will make you fishers of men,' he said. Andrew and Peter must have recognized Jesus for, without hesitation, they left their boat and followed him.

The three men strolled along the shore, talking earnestly together. Suddenly Jesus held up his hand and stared steadily at two other fishermen who were mending their nets along with some others. When he had caught their attention, Jesus murmured, 'Follow me'. Impelled by the wonderful look in Jesus's eyes, the two fishermen left their nets, bade their father farewell, and joined Peter and Andrew beside Jesus. They, too, were brothers, James and John.

The following day, Jesus caught sight of another man, named Philip, who came from Bethsaida where Andrew and Peter also lived. Jesus called Philip to him. Philip it was who introduced to Jesus his next disciple, a worthy man who truly believed in the coming of Christ. This was Nathanael, called by Jesus Bartholomew.

Jesus selected six more men to follow him. Matthew, a tax collector, Thomas, a carpenter like Jesus, Thaddeus, Simon the Canaanite and James the Less, though we know little about these last three men. Finally the twelfth disciple was chosen, Judas Iscariot.

A miracle at a wedding

Ask anyone 'In what respect was Jesus different from other men?'

Some will answer perhaps, 'He was the Son of God.'

Many will reply, 'He could work miracles.'

Yes, today it is generally accepted by all Christians that Jesus could work miracles. But try to imagine the astonishment on the part of the first people who saw Jesus perform his first miracle. It is believed that this took place during the month that Jesus called his first disciples to him.

It seems that Jesus and a few of his followers were once invited to a family wedding in the village of Cana which is not far from Nazareth in Galilee.

The bride and groom must have been friends of Mary, the mother of Jesus, for we are told that she was at the wedding, possibly helping with the preparations.

In those far-off days, weddings were not over and done with in the course of a single day. They were times of great festivity, not only for the bride and groom and their immediate families, but also for all their many relations and friends.

It seems that there were many guests at this particular wedding. There were so many that when Mary cast an anxious eye over their numbers and the jars that contained the wine that was to be drunk, she suspected that the jars would be empty before the last guest departed.

Her doubts were realized. At the height of the merry-making, she was told that the last goblet of wine had been drawn.

Now, this was a very serious matter for the newly-married pair. Once it became known that there was no more wine, the guests would leave, thinking no doubt that their hosts were too mean to provide enough wine for the feast. Not only that, but the festivities would be brought to an abrupt conclusion. This would be a sorry end to a wedding that the bride and groom would remember all their days.

Somebody must have found out that all the wine shops were closed so that it was impossible to buy more wine to refill the jars. What could be done to save the situation and prevent the bride and groom's embarrassment?

Worriedly Mary turned to Jesus. 'How can we help our friends? There is no more wine for the guests.'

He looked at her and quietly nodded, as much as to say, 'Leave this to me.'

Sure that her clever son would think of something, Mary turned to the servants and told them, 'Do whatever Jesus tells you to do as soon as he tells you.'

In a corner of the room stood six large stone water-jars each containing about 75 litres of water. In those days, there was no such thing as running hot and cold water obtainable from taps. All the water needed for a household was stored in large jars.

Much of the water on this day had been used by the guests when they came in from the dusty road. They washed their feet and hands before taking their places at the table. As a consequence, the jars were nearly empty.

Jesus nodded towards them.

'Fill the water jars with water,' he said to the servants. This was no sooner said than done. The servants refilled the jars with cold clear water. Then they returned and looked at Jesus enquiringly.

'Now,' he said, his eyes twinkling, 'fill a tankard and take it to the governor of the feast.'

The governor of the feast would today be called the head waiter.

The tankard, slopping full, was taken to the governor who tasted it. His bearded face lit up with happy surprise. He did not know where it had come from for only Mary and the servants knew that the water-jars had been refilled with water.

'Why, I have never tasted better wine,' he said. Then he looked at the bridegroom. 'Most hosts leave the poorer wine until the wedding feast is nearing its end,' he went on. 'By then the guests do not notice its poor quality so much. But you have served the poorest wine first and kept the best until now. I must congratulate you on your good taste.'

The governor might have been unaware

that a miracle had taken place. But Mary knew and so did the servants.

How they must have whispered together and marvelled at this amazing happening. They surely must have tried to figure out how Jesus had performed such an astonishing feat. For the first time people began to talk, not about Jesus the preacher, but about Jesus the miracle worker.

As for Jesus, we can be sure that he was happy because he had been able to help his friends. We know that he liked to see people happy and that on many occasions he was willing to use his great power to bring happiness.

So it was that a wedding that could have ended in disgrace for the newly-married couple, ended happily, and all because Jesus was there as a wedding-guest.

Healing the sick

There were few places where Jesus could go and not be surrounded by a crowd. The people all hoped that he would start preaching, tell some stories or, perhaps, since he was such a holy man, work a miracle.

Whenever he found the opportunity, Jesus would go up into the mountains. There, it was peaceful and quiet, and he could think clearly and pray to God in peace.

On one occasion, returning from such a rest, Jesus was met by his disciples. Together they started off on the long road to Capernaum.

Further down the road, they came across an unusually large crowd of people who knew Jesus would be passing that way. As they all moved along together, listening to Jesus, they were approached by a leper coming from the direction of Capernaum.

The poor man was a miserable sight. He had bad sores and was greatly disfigured. Because leprosy was incurable as well as infectious it was the law of the land that lepers lived alone or with other lepers.

When the crowd surrounding Jesus saw the leper they moved away in fear. Jesus was left alone in the centre of the road, facing the approaching leper. The crowd gasped as the man went straight up to Jesus. Throwing himself down before him, he begged pitifully, 'Lord, I know you can make me well again if you so wish.'

Jesus, unafraid of the dreaded disease, was immediately filled with sorrow for the poor man. Then he did something which no one else would have dared to do. He put out his hand and actually touched the leper.

The horrified crowd looked on in stunned silence and disbelief as Jesus said, 'Go now and be clean and healthy again.'

Tears of joy streamed down the leper's cheeks as he watched his ugly sores disappear and his body become whole. Then Jesus sent him off saying, 'Do not waste time talking about this to anyone but go straight to the priest in the temple who will examine you and declare you to be healed.

When he arrived in Capernaum, Jesus was approached by a Roman Centurion. Now this really surprised Jesus for the Romans were the rulers of Israel and considered themselves superior to the Jews. A Centurion was an important officer of high rank in the Roman army.

Jesus was even more surprised when the Roman actually knelt in front of him saying, 'Lord, my servant is lying at home very ill and in great pain.'

'Then I will come and heal him,' said Jesus.

'No, Lord,' replied the Centurion. 'I am not worthy that you should come into my house. Just say the word and I know that my servant

will be healed. I am sure you have power over illness, just as I have power to order soldiers to obey my commands.'

On hearing this Jesus was amazed and, turning to his followers, said, 'I have not found even amongst us Jews as much faith as lies in the heart of this officer.' He turned to the Roman and told him to go home. 'For it is because you have such faith in me that you will find your servant healed.'

The Centurion hurried home and there found his servant up and about again, fully recovered. He had been made well at the very moment Jesus said he was cured.

One can be sure that the excited Roman officer must immediately have told all his fellow soldiers and friends about his servant's miraculous cure.

That evening, as news of Jesus and what he was doing spread through the little town, people began to bring their sick and crippled relatives to him. He cured them all without exception, and all the people of Capernaum talked of the wonders Jesus had performed.

Jesus and the Sabbath Day

In the time of Jesus, the day when people rested and went to the Jewish church was called the Sabbath day. Early one fine Sabbath morning, Jesus and his disciples were walking through a corn field. The disciples were all feeling hungry because, according to Jewish law, no one was allowed to eat anything on the Sabbath until after morning service in the synagogue.

As they walked, the disciples could not resist picking the ears of the ripe corn. They rubbed them in the palms of their hands to get rid of the husks, and then ate the grain.

The Pharisees were important people in the Jewish church and very strict where all religious matters were concerned. Some Pharisees were standing at the edge of the field. When they saw what the disciples were doing, they started talking excitedly, and throwing their hands up in horror. One of the many Jewish laws forbade any work to be done on the Sabbath. The Pharisees regarded what the disciples were doing as work. Plucking the ears of corn is just the same as reaping, they argued. Rubbing the husks is no different from threshing. For breaking the religious law, the Pharisees decided that the disciples should be punished!

The Pharisees feared and hated Jesus because what he said sometimes went against their teachings. They watched every move Jesus made, ready to accuse him of the smallest misdeed against the Jewish laws, for they were small-minded men. Somehow or other, one day they would get rid of this man.

Angrily they said to Jesus, 'Look at what your disciples are doing. Don't they know what day it is? Jesus shook his head and replied, 'The Sabbath is meant for man, not man for the Sabbath!'

By this he meant that the Sabbath was a day when people could forget about work and think instead about God and have time to worship him; it was not a time when they had to worry over a lot of rules and regulations about what they could or could not do.

Although the Pharisees did not like Jesus's words, they did not answer. They watched as Jesus and his disciples went on to the synagogue to worship God. Then they fell to talking angrily amongst themselves. There were probably many matters on which they did not always agree, but one thing they were all sure about – this Jesus must be done away with.

As Jesus and his disciples entered the building, Jesus could not help noticing a man with a withered right hand sitting in a corner. The High Priests and Pharisees also noticed how Jesus stopped and looked down at the man's hand.

One of the Pharisees tried to trick Jesus into

saying something that would go against Jewish law. He called out, 'Is it lawful to heal on the Sabbath day?'

Jesus looked at the grim faces of the Pharisees and knew what was in all their minds. But instead of answering, he called to the man saying, 'Stand up and come forward.'

Jesus turned to those around him and asked, 'Is it lawful to help people on the Sabbath day or to hurt them? Is it lawful to save life or to kill?'

The Pharisees moved restlessly and looked at each other. This was the sort of argument they did not like.

'Would any one of you not rescue a sheep of your own if it fell into a pit on the Sabbath?' went on Jesus. 'And how much more is a man worth than a sheep?'

No one answered, but Jesus could tell by the hard looks on their faces that they had no sympathy for the suffering of others.

'Then if you have nothing to say, it must be right to do good deeds on the Sabbath,' Jesus continued angrily, and the Pharisees scowled at him.

Turning to the man with the withered hand, Jesus said quietly, 'Stretch out your right arm.' The man did as he was asked and at once his right hand was made as normal and healthy as his left one. The man stared at it as though he could not believe his eyes. Then he ran from the synagogue to tell his relatives and friends of this miracle. Still the Pharisees kept a sullen silence.

Outside the synagogue a large gathering of Jesus' enemies started a discussion about what they were going to do about him. Jesus left the synagogue and went with his disciples down to the sea. They were not alone, for a great crowd had gathered to hear more of Jesus' teachings and to see the miracles he was working.

The pool at Bethesda

It was the Sabbath day during the period of a religious festival. The streets of Jerusalem were crowded with people who had come to the capital to celebrate.

Jesus and his disciples were there, too. Walking through the city, they came to the pool of Bethesda.

Surrounding the pool were five stone porches. Under them were sheltering many sick and crippled people, all anxiously watching the surface of the water for some sign of movement.

They had heard that, at certain times, an angel would come down and disturb the water. Whoever managed to be the first person to step into the pool after this would be completely cured of whatever sickness or disablement he or she was suffering.

As Jesus passed amongst these poor unhappy people, he caught sight of one man who was stretched out alone on a sleeping mat not far from the edge of the water.

With a pleading expression, the man looked up at Jesus and his friends as they approached. He was probably hoping that one of them would toss him a coin with which he could buy some bread, for he was starving hungry.

Jesus knew that the unlucky fellow had been crippled for 38 years and was unable to move. Year after year he had lain by the pool, hoping that one day he would somehow manage to be first in the water after the angel had disturbed it. During all this time his faith in the story had never faltered.

Feeling great pity for this wretched man who had never lost hope, Jesus asked, 'How would you like to be well again?'

'Sir,' answered the cripple, 'how can I ever be well when I have no one to help me into the pool should the angel disturb the water? I have tried but by the time I reach the edge someone else always manages to get in before me.'

'Get up,' said Jesus firmly. 'Pick up your bed and walk.'

As Jesus spoke, a feeling of strength gradually entered the cripple's body. He rose to his knees and then slowly stood up. He could scarcely believe what was taking place. For the first time in 38 years he had strength in his limbs. He put forward one foot, then the other. He was walking... yes, *walking*! This was a miracle indeed.

Overjoyed at such an instant and amazing recovery, the healed man turned to thank Jesus, but Jesus was nowhere to be seen for he had disappeared into the crowd.

The man rolled up his mat, tucked it under his arm and set off for home to tell his friends what had happened. On the way he was stopped by a group of important-looking Jews. They asked him what he thought he was doing carrying his sleeping mat on the Sabbath.

'He that cured me told me to pick up my mat and walk,' replied the man.

'Who is this man and where is he now?' demanded the Jews. But the healed man could not answer their questions. He did not know Jesus and had not heard about the great

teacher who had come to Jerusalem.

Later that day, the man went into the temple to give thanks. It happened that Jesus noticed him and said, 'Now that you are well, see that in future you live a good life or something worse could happen to you.'

Once he knew that the speaker was Jesus, the cured man rushed off to tell all his friends what had happened as he lay at the side of the pool of Bethesda.

The news soon reached the ears of those Jews who had been asking all the questions earlier on. They lost no time in finding Jesus and accusing him again of breaking the sacred law by working on the Sabbath.

Jesus answered saying, 'My Father works and I must work, too.' This really infuriated the Jews, for not only had Jesus freely admitted working on the Sabbath, but now seemed to be classing himself equal with God. Jesus had gone too far for the Jews, and could no longer be tolerated. They started to discuss plans for ways to put an end to him and his miracles once and for all.

Although Jesus was helping many people, he was also making enemies.

A woman's tears

In matters of behaviour and religion, the Pharisees considered themselves superior to most other people. They were strict with themselves and very unforgiving of people they considered wrongdoers. This is one reason why they were treated as important people in the Jewish Church, and often went around telling others what to do.

One day, Jesus went into the city of Nain. When he arrived, he was met by a certain Pharisee whose name was Simon.

'Would you like to eat at my house tonight?' he asked Jesus. When Jesus accepted the invitation, Simon immediately asked several of his Pharisee friends as well so that they might meet Jesus and question him more closely about what he had been saying and doing. They had heard a lot about Jesus. In their eyes,

he was becoming far too important, and a danger to their authority.

Just as the meal was coming to an end, a woman who was well known in the city for her sinful life, burst into the house and begged to see Jesus. In her hands she held an alabaster jar containing perfumed ointment.

Weeping sadly, she knelt down before Jesus, allowing her tears to fall upon his feet. With her long flowing hair, which she had let down to show everyone she was grief-stricken, she dried his feet and kissed them. Then she poured over them the perfumed ointment.

Stunned and horrified, the Pharisees sat watching in silence. If Jesus has the divine powers he claims, thought Simon, then he should know just how bad this woman really is. How can he sit there allowing her to touch him in this way?

Jesus knew what Simon was thinking. 'Simon, I have something to say to you,' he said.

'Yes, Jesus,' replied Simon. 'I am listening.' He glanced at his friends to make sure they were listening, too.

'There were once two men who needed to borrow money. One borrowed five hundred pence and the other borrowed only fifty pence. When the time came for them to repay the money, they had both fallen on hard times and were unable to do so.

'The man from whom they had borrowed the money took pity on them and, out of the goodness of his heart, forgave them saying they could forget the debts.

'Tell me, Simon, which of these two men do you think had more cause to be grateful?'

Simon was thoughtful. 'I suppose the one who owed the most money,' he replied.

'Of course,' said Jesus. 'Now, I want you to consider this woman. In the past she has done many wrong things but she is sorry for her deeds and wants to be forgiven.

'When I entered your house, you did not give me water so that I could wash my feet, as could be expected by an invited guest. This woman washed them with her tears and dried them with her hair. She kissed me and anointed my feet with precious oil. I tell you that although she has committed many sins she is forgiven.'

Then Jesus turned to the woman saying, 'Go in peace, your faith has saved you.'

Simon felt very ashamed of himself for, as a Pharisee, he realized he had not treated his guest properly, according to the strict rules of his people.

The way Jesus had treated the woman, and the story he told, were both intended to make the Pharisees realize that it does not matter how bad a person has been. Once he is truly sorry and confesses his sins he will be forgiven. Afterwards he will believe in God more firmly than someone who thinks he has never done any wrong. This was something the Pharisees found hard to believe, and their suspicions about Jesus hardened.

The stories Jesus told

Jesus was full of love for everyone, no matter whether they were young or old, rich or poor, sick or healthy. Even if they were wicked he loved them enough to forgive them, especially if they were truly sorry and repented of their evil ways.

Most of all, Jesus liked talking to people and telling them about the Kingdom of Heaven. A lot of what he had to say was difficult for them to understand. Many people could not read or write and so listening to others was the only way they could learn.

Everyone likes a good story, so Jesus told stories to illustrate the lessons he was teaching about God and his Kingdom. This way, not only did people understand but, more important, they remembered what Jesus said. We call these stories 'parables.' These are some of the parables that Jesus told.

A farmer once sowed his field with wheat. When he had finished he was very tired and so went home to bed. That night, while he was sleeping, an enemy came into his field and sowed weeds among the wheat.

At first nothing appeared to be wrong, but as the wheat seed began to grow, so did the weeds. The farmer's servants were puzzled and asked him, 'Sir, did you not sow good seed in your field? Where have all these weeds come from?'

The farmer replied that an enemy must have sown them.

'Would you like us to pull up the weeds for you?' enquired the servants.

'No,' answered the farmer. 'You might uproot some of the wheat at the same time. Let both the wheat and the weeds grow up together until harvest time, then I will tell the reapers to gather the weeds first and burn them. Afterwards they can gather the wheat and put it safely into my barn.'

Jesus explained that the sower of the good seed is like the Son of Man. The field is the world we live in, and the sower of the weeds is the wicked one spreading evil. But God allows both good and bad to grow up side by side until harvest time. Then he will sort everyone out according to how they have behaved.

Another story Jesus told was about the Kingdom of Heaven. The Kingdom of Heaven, he said, was like a treasure hidden in a field. When a man discovered it was there, hidden away, he would go and sell everything he owned. Then, with the money, he could buy the field and be sure of collecting the wonderful treasure for himself.

There was also the story of the merchant who loved pearls. This man was always on the lookout for precious jewels and beautiful pearls. His whole life was spent searching for

something special, despite all he had.

One day he found the most beautiful pearl of all. In his desire to possess it, he sold everything he owned in order to buy this one pearl that he wanted most.

These two stories were told to make the people understand that, if they truly sought after God, they might have to give up many things they treasured. In return, however, they would have the most valuable thing of all – they would belong to the Kingdom of Heaven.

Knowing that several of his disciples were fishermen by trade, Jesus told a little story about the sea.

The Kingdom of Heaven was like a net cast into the sea. When it was full, it was drawn to the shore. In it were all sorts of creatures. Some fish were good for eating, but others were not fit to eat. The fishermen would sit beside the sea sorting the contents of the nets, separating the good fish from the bad, throwing the bad away and keeping the good.

The contents of the net were like all the people in the world – good and bad together. God was like the fishermen who, in the end, would separate the good from the bad and keep the good for himself.

It was with little tales like these that Jesus taught the simple folk who came to him to listen and to learn.

The workers in the vineyard

The sort of things Jesus was saying – strange ideas like 'Forgive your enemies' – had never been said before. But Jesus found that people did not always understand what he was trying to tell them about the Kingdom of God.

One day, he hit upon the idea of making up simple stories about people and things that everyone would be familiar with. These stories, or parables as they are now called, helped people understand and remember the point Jesus was trying to make. This is a parable he told about the owner of a vineyard.

The grapes on the vines had become ripe and were ready for harvesting. According to normal practice in that country, the owner of the vineyard went to the local market first thing in the morning, in order to hire labourers to pick the grapes for him.

In the market square there was a group of men hoping for work. The vineyard owner offered them one penny for a full day's work. In those days, this was considered a very good wage. The labourers were only too pleased to accept and hurried off to the vineyard to get started.

At about nine o'clock, the owner decided he needed more help and so returned to the market place. There he found more labourers looking for work.

'I will pay you fair wages if you will help me with my grape harvest,' he said. They too, were eager to go to the vineyard.

Now the harvest was unusually heavy and at dinner-time the owner of the vineyard realized they would not gather all the harvest that day. He went off and found even more men to help with the picking.

At one hour before the end of the working day, there were still many vines laden with grapes. The vineyard owner returned to the market square yet again and found more men standing idle.

'Why do you stand here all day?' he asked.

'Because no one has hired us for work,' came the reply.

'Well,' said the owner, 'if you hurry to my vineyard and help finish the harvest I will pay what is fair.' So they, too, were employed.

At the end of the day, when the last of the bunches had been picked from the vines, the vineyard owner told his steward to call all the labourers together and pay them their wages. He was to begin with the men who had started last.

The men who had only worked one hour were surprised and delighted to find they had been paid one penny. This was far more than they had expected.

A murmur of surprise ran through the crowd of labourers waiting their turn for payment. 'If he pays them one penny for one hour's work,

what must he be going to pay us?' They asked each other with excitement. But the money paid to them was the same. Just one penny, no more and no less!

Excitement turned to anger. 'This is not fair!' bellowed the men who had worked from early morning until dusk. 'Surely we deserve more than those who have only worked one hour. After all, we have worked right through the heat of the day.'

'So you have,' retorted the owner of the vineyard, 'and you have been paid exactly what we agreed upon this morning. I have not cheated you. I offered you what I considered a fair wage for the job and we struck a bargain which has been fulfilled. I am the owner of this vineyard and I do not intend paying a penny more so you can take your money and go.' There was no answer to this and the grumblers went their way.

By telling this little story, Jesus taught his followers that God, and everything in heaven, is fair. The men who had worked all day were quite happy until they discovered how much those who had only worked one hour were getting. Finding they were not to receive proportionally more, they became angry. They truly believed they had been cheated. But they could not, in all honesty, say they *had* been cheated because they knew they had not.

In the sight of God everyone is equal and should be treated the same, whether he has served God for a whole lifetime, just one day, or even, if it is genuine, for one hour.

Feeding the multitude

Jesus decided it was time his disciples went out on their own to spread the good word, cure the sick, heal the crippled and comfort the suffering. So he sent them off to visit as many places as possible.

Several weeks later, they returned with wonderful stories about what they had been able to do in the name of Jesus. The disciples and Jesus were very tired and in need of rest. Jesus thought it would be a good idea if they all went somewhere peaceful and quiet for a well-deserved break.

Leaving the city, they made their way to the Sea of Galilee. There they took a boat and steered a course towards a quiet part of the shore. Many people had seen them leave the city and had followed them. When the crowd realized that Jesus and his disciples intended to land further along the shore, they hurried to meet them.

Standing up in the boat, Jesus could see the people gathering. He began to feel sorry for them for they were like sheep without a shepherd to lead them.

When the boat came to the shore, Jesus welcomed the crowd. Once the people had settled down, he began to speak to them in his quiet way. By midday, a crowd of five thousand people had assembled to listen to his words.

As evening approached, the disciples came to Jesus and said 'It is getting late and this is a lonely place. Should we not send the people away to the villages so that they can buy food, for they have had nothing to eat?'

Jesus answered saying, 'Why send them away when you can give them all they need? See how much food you can find amongst the crowd.'

Puzzled but obedient, the disciples went amongst the people, but all they could find were five barley loaves and two fishes. These were carried in a basket by a young boy. Willingly the boy handed his food to the disciples saying, 'You are welcome to have them, Sirs.'

Showing the basket to Jesus the disciples said, 'This is all the food we can find. It is not enough for five thousand people.'

'Tell everyone to sit down on the grass in groups of fifty,' said Jesus. Then he took the five loaves and two fishes in his hands and, looking up to heaven, gave thanks and blessed the food. He broke up the bread, cut up the fishes and handed the food to his disciples who, in turn, distributed it amongst the hungry people. Amazingly, the more food they passed out, the more food there seemed to be.

When all had eaten their fill, Jesus said to his disciples, 'Gather up the scraps of food that are left over so that nothing is left to waste.'

To the astonishment of the disciples, they found that when they had collected together the remaining food, they had filled twelve baskets.

The day was over. As they streamed homewards, the crowd spoke excitedly of the wonderful miracle. Five loaves and two fishes had five thousand people! Word of Jesus' miracles spread far and near.

Jesus walks on the water

Surrounded by his faithful disciples, Jesus watched the crowd of five thousand walk slowly away, bound for their homes. But not everyone departed. Some remained and these were Zealots, fanatical Jews, who were sworn to overthrow the rule of the Romans by fair means or foul.

So far these Zealots had been unsuccessful, largely because they lacked a strong leader. Many of them had been amongst the crowd and had watched Jesus perform the miracle of feeding five thousand with only two fishes and five barley loaves. Of course, they knew of Jesus already, and now they decided that here was the very man they needed to lead them in

armed rebellion against the Romans.

The Zealots clustered round Jesus, begging, in fact, demanding that he should lead them in their cause. Sternly Jesus told them to go their ways. 'To turn this unhappy but peaceful land into one of bloodshed?' he queried. 'Jews, Romans, no matter – all are children of God. I refuse to be responsible for shedding one drop of blood, Jewish or Roman.'

He turned to his disciples. 'Climb aboard our boat and cross to the land of Gennesaret where I intend to teach,' said he. 'Meanwhile I will get rid of these people.'

Jesus knew that the Zealots would never leave him to enjoy a day or two of rest. Firmly he turned on them and drove them away. Meanwhile, the disciples were heading across the waters towards Genessaret.

As the sun went down and the sky grew darker, storm clouds began to gather. The wind freshened and began to blow more and more furiously.

Out in the little boat, the disciples were soon in difficulty. The boat was tossed about like a cork and, row as they might, they could make no headway. All through the night they fought to keep the boat afloat.

Suddenly, about four or five o'clock in the morning, when the storm was at its worst, the disciples saw a phantom-like figure walking towards them over the waves. Stricken with fear, they forgot the storm and huddled together, staring wide-eyed at the figure coming closer and closer.

Then the figure spoke. 'Do not be afraid for it is I, Jesus. Be of good cheer.'

Peter was not sure but answered, 'Lord, if it is really you, let me also walk on the water. Then I will know it is you.'

'Come,' said Jesus, and at this Peter stepped out of the boat. He actually walked on the water just like Jesus. But then, looking around, he became aware of the strong wind and rough sea. As fear gripped him once again, he lost faith and began to sink.

'Lord save me!' he cried and Jesus, stretching out his hand, caught him saying, 'Oh Peter, what little faith you have in me. Why did you have doubts?'

When they entered the boat, the storm began to die down, the wind dropped and the sea became calmer. They were all safe.

The madman

By now the disciples were becoming used to the wonderful ways of Jesus. But even so they marvelled as they watched Jesus and Peter walking on the water. What kind of man was this, that even the winds and the sea obeyed him?

The little band landed on a lonely beach. Above them were grassy heights where some swineherds were guarding two thousand pigs. On a nearby hill the disciples saw several tombs, like shallow caves in the hillside.

Suddenly they heard a piercing scream. Out of one of the caves hurtled a near-naked madman. As he raced towards Jesus and the disciples, they saw that manacles which had been fastened to his wrists and ankles were broken. The man had been chained in one of the tombs because of his madness and now he had broken free.

The man flung himself at the feet of Jesus, who looked calmly down at him. 'Out, unclean spirit!' cried Jesus. 'Come out of this man!'

'Ah, do not torment me farther, I beg of you,' wailed the madman.

Jesus repeated his demand to the evil spirits possessing the man. As he did so, the two thousand pigs suddenly rushed over a cliff and drowned in the sea below.

The frightened swineherds all ran to a nearby city. They told their masters that Jesus had driven evil spirits out of a madman into their pigs and that, as a consequence, all the pigs were dead. The owners of the pigs came to Jesus and begged him to leave the neighbourhood before more harm was done.

As though by a miracle, the madman had now recovered his sanity. He asked if he could go with Jesus and his disciples, but Jesus refused. 'Go home,' he said, 'and tell your people what God has done for you and how he had mercy on you.'

A little girl is given life

Shortly after Jesus had cured the madman, he and his friends were walking along followed by the usual large crowd. A well-to-do man pushed his way forward. He knelt at the feet of Jesus. 'Please,' he begged, 'my little daughter is dying. Please, Jesus, come to my house and cure her.'

'Of course I will come with you, Jairus,' said Jesus, recognizing the man. 'Just show me the way.'

As they made to move away together, the crowd closed around them. The disciples tried to protect Jesus from being crushed by all the eager people. Suddenly Jesus stopped, looked around and asked, 'Who touched my robe?'

No one answered. They were all puzzled that Jesus should ask such a question when so many people were jostling him. But Jesus looked steadily about him. Someone needing help had deliberately touched his robe.

At last, a poor woman came forward looking tired and very ill. She was trembling because she was also afraid. 'I touched your robe, Jesus,' she said fearfully. 'I have suffered an illness for twelve years. Doctors have tried many cures but my condition only gets worse. I have heard of your great powers of healing and what you have told people about God. I thought that if only I could touch your robe I would be cured.'

Jesus looked at the woman with a kindly smile. 'Daughter,' he said, 'your faith in me has cured you. Go in peace and be healed.'

As Jesus was speaking to the woman, a servant from Jairus's house came running to his master and with tear-filled eyes cried, 'Master, there is no need to trouble Jesus any more. Your young daughter is already dead.'

Jairus was distraught. It was too late now for Jesus to save his daughter. It seemed to Jairus that Jesus had wasted valuable time curing a poor woman of no consequence, while his own daughter, the child of a rich man, was dying.

'Do not be sad, Jairus,' said Jesus in soothing tones. 'Just believe in me and all will be well.'

He beckoned to Peter, James and John to follow and then set off with the heart-broken Jairus towards his house.

Turning to the crowd, Jesus asked them not to follow them to the house but to stay away. When the small group reached the house, they found everyone crying and wailing in mourning for the young girl.

'Why are you weeping and making all this

fuss?' asked Jesus. 'Don't you know that the little girl is not dead but only sleeping?' Then he turned to her parents and asked them to show him to their daughter's room. There, lying on her bed was the little child, very pale and very still.

Gently, Jesus took her hand in his. 'Wake up, little one,' he said quietly. Immediately the girl sat up, climbed out of bed and walked towards her mother and father who gasped in astonishment. Jesus smiled at the little girl's mother. 'Give the child something to eat. She is well now,' said he.

As he left the house, Jesus instructed Jairus and his wife to tell no one of what had occurred. Jesus did not want simple folk to follow him just to see him work miracles. He wanted them to have faith in God.

A shining light

Whenever it was possible, Jesus would leave the crowds that followed him and go into the hill country. There he was able to pray in peace and quiet.

On one occasion he and his disciples went north to a place called Caesarea Philippi which is at the source of the River Jordan.

Together with Peter, James and John, he climbed high into the mountains. As dusk approached and the air grew cooler, they looked down on the so-called promised land of Israel. It was a beautiful sight in the setting sun.

Very soon it was dark and Jesus prayed to God. Peter, James and John were some distance away, leaning back against a rock. They were very tired after the long climb.

Suddenly Jesus's appearance changed completely. His face shone with a brilliance as bright as the sun and his clothes seemed to blaze with a dazzling whiteness.

As the startled disciples gazed in astonishment, two other figures appeared standing on either side of Jesus. The disciples recognized the figures as Moses and Elijah, the two great leaders from many years ago.

Peter could not hold back. 'Lord,' he cried with nervous excitement, 'let us build three tabernacles here, one for you, one for Moses and one for Elijah.'

As he spoke, a bright cloud came down upon them and a voice from within the cloud said, 'This is my beloved son, listen to what he has to say to you.' Hearing this the disciples were very frightened and fell to the ground hiding their faces in their hands.

Jesus, who knew how afraid they were, touched them saying, 'Stand up, for there is nothing to fear.' The disciples looked up and saw Jesus standing alone. Moses and Elijah had vanished and everywhere was calm and peaceful.

The next day, as they made their way down the mountain, Jesus said, 'Tell no one about the things you have seen until I have risen from the dead.' The disciples gave their promise but they could not understand what Jesus meant about rising from the dead.

When Jesus and his disciples finally reached the bottom of the mountain, they found the usual crowd waiting for Jesus. Instead of the people sitting around patiently, there was a great deal of fuss going on around a boy who was lying on the ground looking very ill.

Seeing Jesus approaching, the boy's father pushed his way through the crowd and came running up to Jesus.

'Master,' he cried in distress, 'my son is deaf and dumb and he has a bad spirit inside him which causes him to have fits. Your good dis-

ciples have tried but they cannot cure him. If you can do anything, please help us.'

Jesus replied, 'All things are possible to those who believe.' In tears, the boy's father cried out 'Lord, I believe!'

Then Jesus commanded the bad spirit to leave the boy. At first the lad tossed about screaming and moaning on the ground. Quite suddenly, he stopped and lay there as if he were dead.

Jesus went forward and, taking the boy by the hand, helped him to stand up. The crowd could see immediately that he had been cured. They gasped in amazement.

Once again Jesus had performed an astounding miracle and his fame spread wider.

Jesus and the sick man

Whenever Jesus spoke about the Kingdom of Heaven, his disciples were never quite sure what it would be like. They thought that as Jesus was King of the Jews and had been sent to save them, he would one day be like any other king but with a great deal more power. By working a really big miracle, Jesus would eventually conquer not only the Romans but the rest of the world as well. And he would do all this without anyone being hurt.

Jesus might, they thought, set up his capital there in Jerusalem. He would then sit in majesty, surrounded by governors who would help him rule his empire. Among these people they imagined themselves having all the important jobs, such as Prime Minister, Treasurer, Head of the Church, Lord Justice and so on.

Often the disciples would argue about which of them would be the most important. Once, when they were walking some way behind Jesus, he overheard them arguing. Afterwards he called them all together and asked them what they were talking about.

At first they were ashamed to tell him. Then one stood up and asked, 'Master, who is to be the greatest among us in the Kingdom of Heaven?'

Nearby a little child was playing. Jesus called to him to come and stand exactly where he had been sitting so it looked as if the child was the one who was preaching. Jesus then said, 'Unless you all stop this arguing about who should be the greatest, none of you will be able to enter the Kingdom of Heaven. If any of you want to be really great, you must first become like this little child, humble and willing to serve other people. In my kingdom the greatest ones will be those who serve and not those who expect people to wait on them.'

Whilst Jesus was in the countryside, many people brought their children to him so that, when he had finished preaching, he might bless them. On one occasion, a number of children came and were all running around making rather a lot of noise. The disciples thought they might be annoying Jesus and ordered them to go away saying, 'Do not come bothering Jesus. He is much too busy with more important matters.'

When Jesus saw and heard what was happening he told his disciples to stand back, saying, 'Let the little children come to me and do not forbid them. I tell you, no one will enter the Kingdom of Heaven who is not as trusting and obedient and humble as a child.' Having said that he gathered all the children to him and blessed each one in turn.

As Jesus and his disciples left the place where they had been staying to journey on their way, a young man came running up. Kneeling before Jesus he said, 'Good Master, what must I do that I may have eternal life?'

'Why do you call me good?' asked Jesus. 'No one is *good* but God. You have been taught the scriptures and you have learnt the Commandments. Do you keep them?'

The young man answered saying, 'Yes, Master. I have learnt the scriptures and know all the Commandments and ever since I was small I have always obeyed them.'

Jesus looked into the young man's eyes and knew that he meant well. He liked him and thought he would probably make a very good disciple. Jesus also knew that the man was very rich. Rich people, he thought, usually trust more in riches than in God.

'There is only one thing you lack,' Jesus said to the young man. 'You must go and sell everything that you have. Then give all the money you receive to the poor. That way you shall have treasure in heaven. When you have done this come back and follow me, for I have work for you to do.'

Hearing this the young man turned away sadly. He had great riches and very many possessions, and he could not bear to sell them or give them away. These things meant too much to the young man. Jesus, too, was sad that this man, who could have done good work for God, thought so much of his worldly goods that he could not bring himself to part with them.

Turning to his disciples, Jesus said, 'How hard it is for a rich man to enter the kingdom of God.' The disciples were very surprised to hear this. Jesus went on, 'How hard it is for those who trust only in riches to enter the Kingdom of Heaven. It is easier for a camel to go through the eye of a needle than for a rich man to enter the Kingdom of God.'

The disciples could not understand this at all. They knew that everyone would like to have money and most people hoped that one day they would be rich.

A person who spends most of his time thinking about money is usually selfish, often dishonest and gives little time to thinking of God. But someone who works hard and gets rich honestly, yet who is also unselfish and trusts in God, will be able to enter the kingdom of God.

Jesus was explaining that all people, whether they are rich or poor, would have to be as trusting and obedient as a child if they were to enter God's Kingdom.

The good Samaritan

One day when Jesus was talking to a crowd of people, a crafty lawyer stood up and tried to trick him by getting him to say things which were against the Jewish law.

'Tell me what I must do to gain everlasting life?' he asked.

'Surely you, a lawyer, must know the answer to that,' replied Jesus. 'What is written in your law books?'

Fearing that the crowd might think he did not know the Jewish teachings, the lawyer answered quickly, 'You should love the Lord your God with all your heart and with all your soul and with all your strength and with all your mind and you should love your neighbour as you love yourself!'

'That is right,' said Jesus. 'You have answered your own question. Do that and you will gain eternal life.'

Realizing he had been made to look silly by answering his own question, the lawyer persisted in questioning Jesus still farther, hoping he would eventually say the wrong thing.

'Who is my neighbour?' came his next question.

'Listen to my story,' said Jesus, 'then perhaps you will find out.

'There was once a certain Jew travelling on the road from Jerusalem to Jericho. Half way between the two cities he was attacked and beaten up by a band of thieves.

'They made off with all he had, including most of the clothes he was wearing. He was left wounded and bleeding by the roadside.

'After a short while a priest, who had been teaching people about the love of God, came hurrying by. He saw the man lying in such a terrible state but chose to ignore him. Crossing to the other side, the priest continued on his way.

'A little while later a Levite came upon the unfortunate Jew and he too pretended not to see him lying there.

'There next came a Samaritan who was one of a people greatly despised by the Jews. Nobody would ever expect a Samaritan to stop for a Jew but this one did, for he felt pity for the wretched man lying there on the ground.

'Dismounting from his ass, he cleansed the man's wounds with oil and wine, then bound them up with cloth. He put the man on his ass and, walking beside, took him to the nearest

inn where he continued to care for him.
'The next day, as the Jew was still too ill to be moved, the Samaritan left enough money with the inn-keeper to pay the expenses of looking after the sick man. "If there is not enough here, I will repay you when I return," he said.'

Then Jesus turned to the lawyer. 'Which of the three men was the true neighbour of the one attacked by the thieves?' he asked.

The lawyer had to answer 'The Samaritan.'

The Prodigal Son

The Pharisees and Scribes hated Jesus and hoped one day to see an end of him. They could not help noticing that Jesus spent much time with people that everyone knew were sinners. 'Why do you, who claim to be the Son of God, choose to talk and even eat meals with such bad people?' they asked him.

Jesus knew that these men were his enemies and would never befriend him. Even so, he tried to make them understand how God was like the shepherd who goes out of his way to save one sheep that has strayed from the flock. 'Let me explain farther by telling you a story.'

'One day, the younger son went to his father and said, "Please father, could I now have my share of the money I will one day inherit? I am tired of living here and want to travel."

'Although the old father did not want to see him leave, he gave the boy what he wanted. A few days later the boy said farewell to his unhappy father and to his brother who was angry because he was leaving. He travelled to a distant land where he soon found a life of pleasure.

'It did not take long for the young man to spend all the money he had, and he was soon looking for a job.

'Now it just so happened that a terrible famine developed in the land. Food became very scarce and work difficult to find. The only job the youth could find was looking after a farmer's pigs.

'At times he was so hungry he could have eaten the very husks that were fed to the pigs. No one gave him any food nor cared particularly what happened to him. At last he came to his senses and realized how foolish he had been.

' "My father's servants have more bread than they can eat, yet here I am starving!" he thought. "I will go home to my father and ask him to forgive me. Then I will beg him to let me work as a hired servant for him for I am no longer worthy to be called his son."

'So he set off for home. After a long and exhausting journey he came in sight of his old home. When the boy was still some distance from the house, his father saw his weary, tattered son approaching. In spite of his changed appearance he recognised him at once.

' "My son, my son" he cried, his eyes streaming with tears of happiness. He ran to greet him, throwing his arms around his neck.

' "Father," said the younger son, "I have let you down, I have led a very wicked life and wasted all the money you gave me. I am no longer fit to be called your son."

'The father put an arm about his son's shoulders. He called to his servants, saying, "Bring out the best robe for my son, a ring for his finger and shoes for his feet. Kill the fattened calf so that we can have a feast, for my son was lost and now he is found and we shall all make merry."

'Now the elder son, who had been at home with his father all this time, had worked hard and never caused any trouble. On his way back from the fields that evening he heard the sounds of dancing and music. He called to one of the servants asking, "What is going on?"

'"Don't you know?" replied the servant. "Your younger brother has returned home and your father has killed the fattened calf."

'At hearing this the elder son became angry and refused to go into the house.

'"Why won't you come in and welcome your lost brother?" asked his father who had come out, looking for him.

'"I have worked here with you all the time my young brother has been away enjoying himself. Not once have I caused you trouble, yet you have killed our fattened calf for that ne'er do well. You never once arranged a party for me and my friends," replied the elder son.

'"My son," said the man, "you are always with me, and all that I have will be yours one day. But today we must be happy because my other son, your only brother, who was lost has been found. He was dead but is alive again." '

Jesus glanced at his listeners. 'Have mercy on those who have sinned,' he said, 'for in the eyes of the Lord *all* men are his children.'

The Tax Collector

Excitement was mounting everywhere as news of Jesus and his amazing miracles spread far and wide. Wherever he went, huge crowds gathered to see him and listen to the wonderful stories he was telling.

Not everyone liked what he said. Some people, especially those in authority, were worried that his words might cause trouble for them.

Other people were made to think again about their own bad ways. Others were comforted and reassured. No one was ever bored.

Curiosity about what this amazing man might do or say next attracted most people to Jesus. But to the sick, the crippled, and those troubled by guilty consciences, Jesus meant a great deal more. To these poor, suffering people he offered the hope of being cured.

One day, Jesus visited the city of Jericho where a man named Zacchaeus (say Zac-e-us) was the chief tax collector for the Roman Government. The Romans had conquered the country, making it part of their enormous Empire. Caesar, the ruler of the Roman Empire, had declared that everyone had to pay taxes to Rome.

Nobody likes paying taxes. The Jews in particular hated paying their conquerors, because the Romans were already taking the best that their country produced for themselves.

Tax collectors, like Zacchaeus, were also hated. This was particularly because some of them would cheat poor people. Those who could not read and write often found they were paying more than they should have done. Then the tax collectors kept the extra money for themselves.

Needless to say, Zacchaeus was extremely wealthy. But for all his money, he was not a happy man. Everyone loathed him and few people would even bother to talk to him.

When Zacchaeus heard that Jesus was coming to Jericho, like everyone else, he wanted to see what this great teacher was like. But he was only a small man, not tall enough to see over heads of people in the crowd. He also knew that no one would make way so that a hated tax collector should be able to see Jesus.

Zacchaeus then had an idea. If he climbed a tree that overhung the road along which Jesus would pass, he would see everything. He soon found a suitable tree, scrambled up, and sat on a branch that gave him the best view of all the traffic.

Very soon Jesus appeared surrounded by his friends and followers. To Zacchaeus's great surprise, he stopped directly underneath the branch on which Zacchaeus was sitting. Looking up, Jesus beckoned to the tax collector to come down, saying, 'Today I want to stay in your house.' Somehow, Jesus knew that Zacchaeus was troubled and needed his help as much as anyone else.

Zacchaeus, overjoyed, nearly fell out of the tree with excitement. The people gathered around were upset that Jesus should even talk to a wicked tax collector. They were even more shocked that he chose to be a guest in the house of such a sinner.

On the doorstep of his house, Zacchaeus stopped and, turning to Jesus, said in a loud voice so that everyone in the crowd could hear, 'Lord, I am now going to give half my goods to the poor and if I have cheated anyone by taking more from them in taxes than they should have paid, then from what I have left, I will pay back four times the amount I took.'

Jesus was pleased to hear this and said to the crowd, 'Today salvation has come to this house. Zacchaeus was guilty and in need of forgiveness for his sins, just as many of you are. The Son of Man has come to seek and save people like him who have lost their way.'

Zacchaeus smiled and looked happy for the first time in his life. The crowd were pleased too and asked Jesus to tell them one of his famous stories. So Jesus told them about a certain nobleman who was called away to another country to receive a kingdom and crown. Before he left he gave a talent, (which was a valuable coin of the time) to each of his servants saying, 'Stay here until I return.'

When the nobleman had been given his new kingdom, he returned and called his servants together. He asked each one in turn what he

had done with his talent.

The first servant said he had worked hard at trading and now had ten talents. The nobleman was very pleased and said he would make him ruler over ten cities.

The next servant had also traded but had only managed to make five talents. The nobleman was again pleased and promised he should be made ruler over five cities.

The third servant said he still had his master's talent, having buried it in the ground. He added that he did not think his master should make a profit from something he had not worked for.

The nobleman was very angry and instructed that the talent be taken from him and given to the servant who had made ten talents.

The nobleman had placed trust in his servants. To those who had done according to his wishes and succeeded, he had given more. To him that had not, he had taken away even the talent that he had first given.

Jesus told this story to explain that, when God gives a person the ability to do something, he must use that ability for the good of himself and others. If he idles his time and does nothing, he is wasting his gift and God will eventually take it from him. For it is true that practice makes perfect, whilst idleness leads to waste.

The raising of Lazarus

Near Jerusalem, in the little village of Bethany, there lived a man named Lazarus and his two sisters, Mary and Martha. All three were close friends of Jesus.

One day Lazarus was taken ill. He was so ill that his sisters feared he might die. So they sent a message to Jesus hoping he could find time to come and cure their poor sick brother.

When the message finally reached Jesus, he was a long way away with his disciples. For some reason he could not leave for Bethany immediately. Several days passed before he could go there. When at last he and his disciples arrived in Bethany, Lazarus had died and been in his tomb for four days.

Martha and Mary told Jesus that, had he been able to come a few days sooner, their brother would not be dead. They added that they knew that whatever Jesus asked of God, God would give to him. Surely he could do something?

'Your brother will rise again,' Jesus replied.

'For whoever believes in me will have everlasting life.'

The sight of the sisters' tears made Jesus very sad and he asked, 'Where have you laid him?' They led Jesus to the tomb. It was a cave with a large stone rolled across the entrance to close it. Outside the tomb many friends of Lazarus had gathered.

'Take the stone away,' said Jesus. Then he knelt and prayed for God's help to perform a miracle. Jesus knew that without his father's approval, he would not have the power to raise Lazarus from the dead.

When he had finished praying, Jesus called out in a loud voice, 'Lazarus, come forth.' Lazarus, who had been dead, awoke and came out of the tomb, shielding his eyes from the sunlight.

Most of the Jews who saw this miracle now believed that Jesus was truly the Son of God. But those who still did not believe could not wait to get back to Jerusalem to tell the Pharisees what had happened.

Immediately the Pharisees called a meeting to discuss what should be done about this man Jesus, whose teaching and miracles they feared. And so the plot to get rid of Jesus was finally hatched.

The man born blind

One day as Jesus and his disciples were walking along, they came upon a blind man sitting begging just outside the main entrance of a temple. The disciples all knew this man and one of them asked as he turned to Jesus, 'Master, who did sin, this man or his parents, so that he was born blind?' (In those days people believed that any deformity or illness was a punishment for sin.)

'Neither,' answered Jesus. 'This man is not being punished for anything his parents might have done, nor is he himself a very sinful person. God has allowed him to be blind and to live his life until now in darkness so that I might give him sight, and in so doing show to you the mighty power of God. For as long as I

am in the world, I am the light of the world.'

After uttering these words Jesus spat on the ground. He mixed the saliva with the earth to make a little paste which he placed gently on the man's eyes. 'Go and wash in the pool of Siloam,' he told him.

Mystified, the man was led to the pool where he washed his eyelids and on opening them gazed in wonder about him. A miracle had been performed. He could see!

'What has happened to you?' all his friends asked. 'How is it that you can now see?' He told them how it had happened.

Amazed at what had taken place, the people hurried him off to the temple so the Pharisees might know of this great miracle. As usual the Pharisees asked many searching questions which the healed man answered as well as he could.

At last they put a question to the man who had been blind asking, 'What do you think of this man who has given you your sight?'

'I think he is a prophet,' came the reply.

This answer really confused the Pharisees. Perhaps the beggar was lying. Could it be that he had never been blind at all? They sent for his parents. 'Is this your son whom you say was born blind, and how is it that he can now see?' they questioned.

The parents were very frightened of the Pharisees and answered warily, 'Yes. This is our son. Ask anyone and they will tell you he was born blind and has been blind all his life. We do not know anything about how he came to receive his sight, but why do you not ask him?'

The Pharisees turned to the son and asked again, 'How did this man, who you say is a Prophet, but we know is called Jesus, give you your sight?'

By this time the poor fellow was becoming sick and tired of repeating answers to the same questions.

'I have already told you,' he snapped. 'Why do I have to tell you again and again? Do you want to become his disciples, too?'

The Pharisees were furious. 'We are the disciples of Moses,' they thundered. 'We know God spoke to Moses but as for this fellow Jesus, no one knows where he comes from.'

To this the man replied: 'That is the wonderful thing. You know not where he comes from yet he opened my eyes. Nobody before has heard of anyone opening the eyes of a blind man. If this man was not sent by God he could have done nothing.'

Outraged, the Pharisees leapt to their feet and threw the beggar out of the temple. On hearing what had happened, Jesus went in search of the beggar. When they met, he asked, 'Do you believe in the Son of God?'

'Who is he that I might believe in him?'

'He now speaks to you,' came the reply. At this, the man knelt down before Jesus.

'Lord, I believe,' he said.

The man who was deaf

The more Jesus did to help people, so the more his fame spread and the more his enemies grew jealous of him. It was the people with positions of power in the Jewish church who always seemed to be against him. Most of them, lacking the courage to argue with Jesus face to face, preferred the more cowardly way. They tried to trick Jesus into saying things against the Jewish faith. They hoped that this would upset the people and turn them against him. The enemies of Jesus tried to make life difficult for him. All Jesus wanted to do was to teach the truth to anyone who would listen.

On one occasion, Jesus and his disciples left Galilee and started out on what was in those days a very long journey. This time the little party went north to the port of Tyre which is on the Mediterranean sea coast of Upper Galilee.

The people in that part of the country had not heard very much about Jesus and his wonderful work. Most of them did not follow the same strict religious beliefs as the Jews, and they were known as Gentiles. The Jews rather looked down on the Gentiles, and many Jews chose to have nothing to do with them.

Jesus and his faithful disciples found a house in Tyre where they could stay for a while without being bothered by their enemies. Probably, as they relaxed, they talked about where they were going and all the work that lay ahead in the following weeks.

A certain woman living in Tyre had heard of the miraculous cures that Jesus had been performing. She found out that he was staying in the port. After asking a few people where she could find Jesus, the woman finally discovered the house where he was staying and called at the door. Once inside, she threw herself at Jesus's feet, begging him to remove an evil spirit that had taken possession of her poor daughter.

At first Jesus said he could do nothing for the woman's daughter. He had to look after the needs of his own people, the Jews, before he could attend to the people of other nationalities. This was unusual for Jesus for it was not his custom to refuse aid to anybody in need.

The woman insisted, saying, 'But, Master, you have helped many Jews, surely you can spare just a little help for my poor daughter?' Finally Jesus relented. He was so impressed by the polite and humble way the woman had asked him that he said, 'Go home and you will find your daughter healed.'

The woman thanked Jesus with all her heart. She hurried home to find her daughter lying peacefully on her bed, quite free of the evil spirit.

After this, Jesus decided to go even farther north to the port of Sidon. He would then journey inland, returning to Galilee by way of Decapolis, a smaller country which lay on the other side of the River Jordan.

News that Jesus was in the country soon spread through the towns and villages of Decapolis. Before long, he and his disciples were met by a crowd of people who had with them a man who was deaf and almost dumb. His friends had brought him to Jesus in the hope Jesus would cure him, just as he had cured the girl who had been possessed of an evil spirit.

They begged Jesus to help their poor friend. He could not hear and had such difficulty in speaking he could not make people understand him.

Jesus could see the man was very nervous, so he took him aside from the crowd. He put his fingers gently in the man's ears, and touched the man's tongue with spittle. Then, looking up to heaven, Jesus said, 'Be opened.'

Almost immediately, the man who was deaf and dumb changed. His ears cleared and, for the first time in his life, he heard the sound of people's voices, and all the different noises going on around him. When he opened his mouth to speak, the words came out clearly and distinctly instead of being mumbled sounds. At last the man could speak and be understood. A new life had been opened to him.

Jesus said to the excited but grateful man, 'Now go on your way, but do not tell anyone what took place or how you obtained your hearing and speech.'

The man went on his way but it is not difficult to understand that he found it impossible to keep quiet. He just could not stop talking about the miracle Jesus had performed. Before long, news had spread over a wide area and people came flocking to see Jesus, to hear him preach, and hoping to see more miracles.

Now it had been foretold by the prophets that, when the Messiah came to earth, he would have power to unstop the ears of the deaf and be able to unloose the tongues of the dumb so that they would be able to sing. When news of this new miracle reached other parts of the country, many Jews said to each other, 'This is proof that Jesus is the promised Messiah, the Saviour whom God has promised us.' And his enemies listened... and waited.

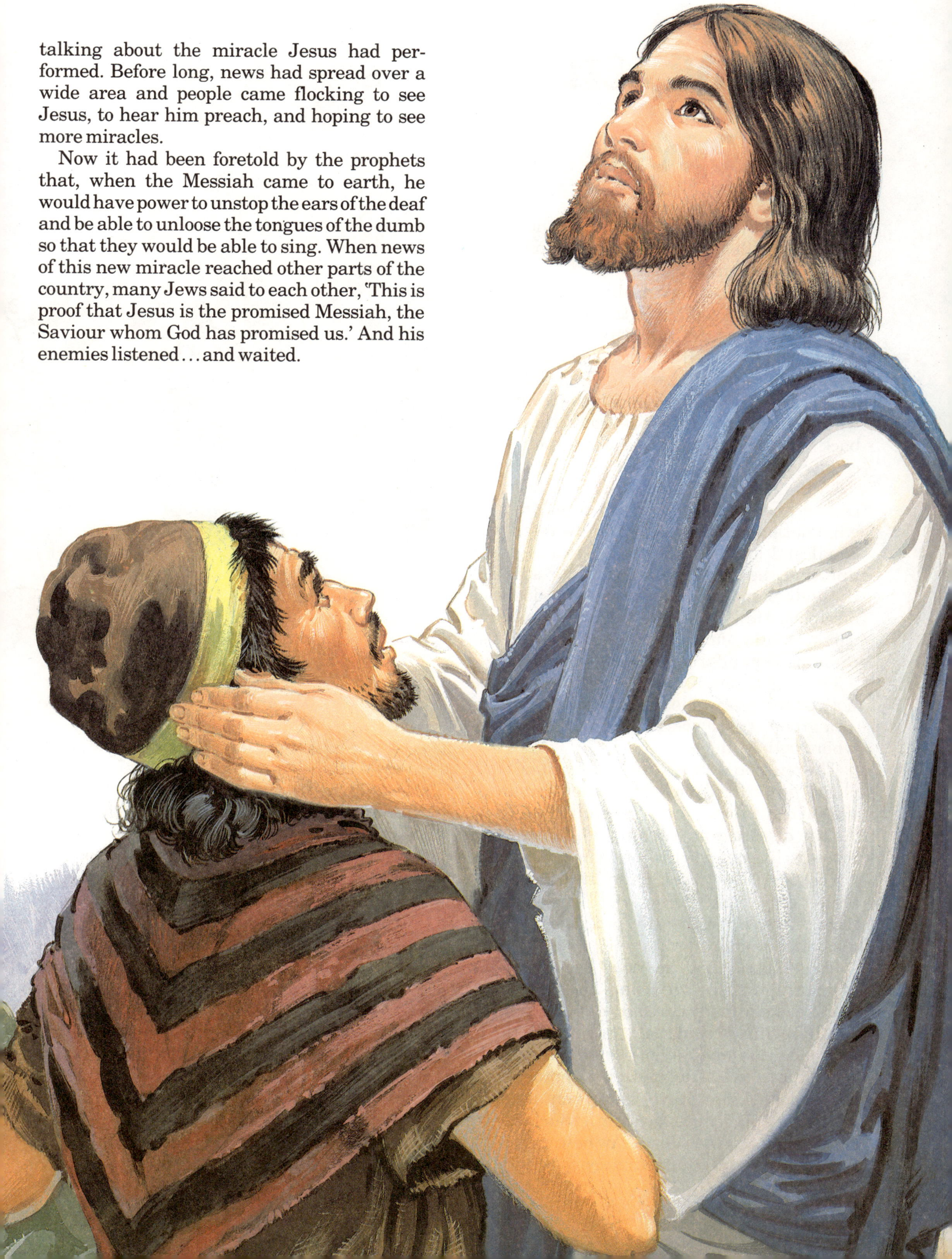

The ten lepers

Jesus and his disciples were making their way through Galilee, towards Samaria, on their way to Jerusalem.

Samaria lay between Galilee in the north and Judea in the south, and the Jews of Galilee and Judea hated the Samaritans. Most Jews, rather than pass through Samaria, would often take a much longer route from Galilee to Judea. They would cross the River Jordan into what is now the country of Jordan, then cross back again farther south into their own country.

Unlike many people, Jesus was not concerned about where a person came from or what nationality he was. To him everyone was equal and just as important. So calmly and unafraid, he took the short route straight through Samaria, followed by his doubtful disciples. How could they be sure no harm would befall them? But they put their trust in their master and trudged along in his wake.

Passing through a certain village, Jesus noticed ten miserable men standing together in a group. There was no one to be seen elsewhere in the village.

The ten men were covered in sores, and were clearly suffering from leprosy, the terrible disease which afflicted many people in those days. As the disease was catching, all lepers were forced to live outside the towns in wild parts of the country. They had to carry little hand bells which they rang, calling out, 'Unclean! Unclean!' This warned healthy people to keep well away from them.

These lepers had heard of Jesus and the wonderful work he was doing. They also knew that he had already cured one leper simply by touching him. Would he do the same for them. It is easy to imagine how excited they were when they saw his stately figure approaching.

'Jesus, Master, have mercy on us poor lepers,' one of them begged him, stretching out wasted hands. When Jesus saw how these men were suffering he immediately took pity on them and said, 'Go and show yourselves to the priests.'

The law at that time stated that should a leper become cured, he must immediately show himself to a priest, who would pronounce him free of the disease. Only after the priest had declared a leper to be free of the dreaded disease, could that person once again mix with healthy people. This did not often take place for leprosy was usually incurable.

The lepers could hardly believe their ears but, hoping against hope, they hurried towards the temple. As they ran they noticed that their horrible sores were disappearing, leaving their bodies clean and healthy again. How overjoyed they were at the thought of being back in their homes, free to live a normal life once more.

Suddenly one of the ten stopped in his tracks, turned and ran back to where Jesus and his disciples were standing. He flung himself at Jesus's feet and gave thanks for the cure.

Jesus answered sadly, saying, 'Were there not ten of you who were made well? What has happened to the other nine?' The man could only shake his head. He looked gratefully up into the gentle eyes of the man who had saved him. Jesus took his hands and raised him to his feet and bade him stand straight.

'Go your way,' said Jesus. 'Your faith has made you whole.' The man ran after his companions to scold them and remind them that they had been cured by the marvellous power of the Great Healer.

The woman at the well

As you have read in the previous story, the Jews of Galilee and Judea detested the Samaritans. For one thing, the Samaritans had intermarried with foreign races, something the Jews refused to do. For another, there were certain religious differences between the two peoples. It all added up to the fact that the Jews despised the Samaritans. (This gives added point to Jesus's parable about the good Samaritan related elsewhere in this book).

In return, as you might expect, there was no love lost on the part of the Samaritans for the Jews of Galilee and Judea. For example, a Jew who decided to brave the hatred of the Samaritans, and to cross Samaria for some reason or other, would quite likely be refused bread and water by the Samaritans.

All of this leads us on to the next story of Jesus.

It was as he and his disciples were continuing their journey across Samaria that they came to rest at Jacob's Well. Nearby was the Samaritan city of Sychar.

The disciples went on into the town, hoping to find a shopkeeper who would sell them some food. Jesus, feeling very weary, sat at the side of the well to rest.

The well was very deep and water could only be reached by a bucket let down by a rope. Most travellers carried a bucket with them, but Jesus had no bucket and was therefore unable to quench his thirst.

He had been resting for a little while when he saw a Samaritan woman walking gracefully towards him. She had a large ewer in one hand and was obviously coming to draw water from the well.

Jesus smiled at her and quietly asked her if she would give him a drink of water. Her eyes opened wide with amazement.

'Are you not a Jew,' she asked, 'from Judea or Galilee?'

'Even so,' replied Jesus.

'Yet you ask me, a woman of Samaria, to give you a drink? Why? Usually you Jews are too proud and unfriendly to have anything to do with Samaritans.'

'That is so,' replied Jesus. 'But you do not know who I am. Had you known, before I could have asked you for water, you would have asked *me* to give *you* living water rather than the other way around.'

This remark puzzled the woman.

'Sir,' said she, 'you do not have a bucket. The well is deep and so you are unable to draw water for yourself. How then could you offer me water, living, whatever that might mean, or otherwise?' Before Jesus could answer her, she went on:

'You say I do not know you? Very well, *who* are you? Do not tell me that you are someone greater than Jacob who drank here himself – yes, and his children after him – and left the well to us Samaritans that we may never need be thirsty.'

Jesus shook his head. He gestured towards the well. 'Whoever drinks *this* water will soon thirst again,' he said. 'But whoever drinks the water that *I* shall give will never be thirsty again.'

Jesus meant that by the knowledge that he could give her, her soul would be refreshed just as her body was refreshed by water. But the simple woman did not understand what he was saying. She thought that by some wonderful means he could give her a drink of special water. By drinking it, she would never be thirsty again, nor have to go to the well to carry back a heavy ewer. So she asked Jesus to give her some of this special water that she would never be thirsty again.

To make her understand and realize that he was not an ordinary man, Jesus then went on to tell her certain secret things about herself. She was startled. *Now* he was talking about something she *did* understand. How could he have known these secret matters? There was only one answer.

'You are a prophet given to second sight,' she cried. Then, changing the subject, she pointed to a nearby Samaritan temple. 'Our ancestors worshipped there,' said she, 'but you Jews say that all men must worship at the Temple in Jerusalem.'

'Only one thing really matters,' Jesus said, 'that all men should worship God in their

hearts.' He went on to explain to her his mission on earth. At last she stared at him with wonder in her eyes. 'You are the Christ whose coming has been foretold,' she murmured very quietly.

The disciples, returning from their quest for food, were amazed to find Jesus deep in conversation with a Samaritan woman. Just as they arrived, the woman took her leave and hurried back to the town of Sychar. She told all her friends there about the wonderful teacher who was resting at the well. Many of them flocked to listen to him. They hailed him truly as the Son of God, the Saviour of the World, and begged him to remain with them and teach them more about God.

But Jesus could only stay two days. There was much more for him to do in the short space of time left to him on earth.

Palm Sunday

Jesus and the disciples travelled on to Jerusalem, which was at that time crowded with Jews who had arrived from near and far for the great Passover festival. They had reached a hill called the Mount of Olives, when Jesus pointed to a village nearby.

'I'd like two of you to do something for me,' he told his friends. 'If you go to the village you'll find a donkey and her colt tied up by the first house. Untie the colt and bring it to me.'

'But what if anyone stops us?' they asked him.

'Tell them that the master needs it,' he answered, 'and there'll be no problem.'

The two disciples went at once and found the colt as Jesus had described. They were just about to take it when a bystander demanded to know what they were doing. When they said that the master needed it, the man nodded and let them carry on.

They led the colt to the place where Jesus and the other disciples were waiting. First, they threw some clothes over its back and then Jesus sat on it. Although no one had ridden it before, it stood calmly and was not at all restless. The words that the prophet Isaiah had written about the Messiah hundreds of years before were coming true: 'Jerusalem, your king is coming humbly to you, riding on a colt.'

Many of the people who were in Jerusalem for the Passover festival had heard about Jesus. The word quickly spread that he was approaching the city and would soon be arriving. It wasn't long before crowds gathered in the streets along which they thought he would enter the city. They believed that he was coming as their king, the Messiah, so they cut palm branches and prepared to welcome him.

As soon as they saw Jesus riding up the street, a great cheer went up. 'Praise God!' they shouted. Son of David, save us! Long live the King of Israel! Long live the one who comes in God's name!'

They waved the palm branches and spread them on the ground, together with clothing, to make a carpet for their king to ride over. The sound of their rejoicing echoed around the streets and buildings of Jerusalem. People who had never heard of Jesus began to ask questions about him, and those who knew him talked about the wonderful things he had said and done. Only the religious leaders of the city were unhappy, because they did not believe that he was the Son of God, the Messiah, and they didn't want the people following him. 'Tell them to stop shouting those things,' they asked Jesus.

'I cannot do a thing,' he told them. 'If they stopped, even the stones of the city would cry out!'

Jesus was thankful for the welcome the people gave him, but he knew that within a week another crowd would be shouting for his death. With these mixed feelings Jesus rode right into the centre of the city and spent some time looking around the great Temple. Towards evening he and the disciples left and returned to Bethany where they were staying.

Later on, Jesus' friends remembered some words written many years before by the prophet Zechariah:

> 'People of Jerusalem, rejoice and shout for joy!
> See how your King comes to you:
> He is great, yet he is humble,
> For he rides on a donkey to meet you.'

The next day Jesus and the disciples went into the city again and walked straight to the Temple. When Jesus had looked around it the day before, he had been very upset at what he saw.

In the outer courtyard there were large numbers of traders doing their business with the travellers who were in Jerusalem for the Passover. The traders sold pigeons and other animals which people needed for the sacrifices they made in the Temple services. The trouble was that the traders charged more than they should have done. When people paid money to the Temple officials, they had to use special Jewish coins instead of the usual Roman ones, so there were several stalls where Roman money could be exchanged for these special coins. Many of the traders cheated people by

not giving them enough for their money. All this angered Jesus so much that he stormed into the courtyard, shouting at the traders to get out at once.

There was a great commotion as he turned over the tables and seats used by the swindlers, scattering their money all over the ground. The traders knew that Jesus was popular with many people, so they left quickly with Jesus calling after them. 'God said, "My house should be a house of prayer;" you have made it nothing but a den of robbers.'

Jesus is betrayed

Jesus was now the most popular man in the whole of Israel. Every day that he taught in the Temple, people flocked to hear him speak. This so infuriated the Chief Priests that they plotted to destroy Jesus.

Judas Iscariot, one of Jesus's disciples, got to hear of their plans. He went to the priests and asked them how much they would be prepared to pay him to betray Jesus. The priests offered Judas Iscariot only thirty pieces of silver. This was the price normally paid for a slave.

The time was just before the Feast of the Passover. Since Jesus had no house of his own, there was nowhere that he and his followers could prepare a Passover feast. Jesus secretly arranged for a room to be made available that would be safe from their enemies.

On the day of the feast, Jesus said to Peter and John, two of his disciples, 'Go into Jerusalem and you will see a man carrying a pitcher of water. Follow him to his house and he will show you a large upstairs room. Make this ready for the rest of us who will follow at dusk.'

Everything happened exactly as Jesus had said. They all gathered for what was to be the last supper Jesus would eat on with his disciples.

When the meal was ready, Jesus blessed the bread and wine and gave it to his disciples. It was a sad time for him for he knew what was to happen after the supper.

As they ate, Jesus said, 'One of you is about to betray me.' Shocked and dismayed, the disciples gathered around Jesus, denying they would ever betray him. But as they spoke, Judas Iscariot slipped out. He hurried off to see the High Priest, and there he offered to lead the

soldiers to capture Jesus.

'Before this night is out you will all have been disloyal to me,' Jesus went on.

'Not me,' protested Peter. 'Everyone else may be disloyal but I will follow you to prison and death.'

Sadly, Jesus replied 'This very night, before the cock crows you will deny having known me three times.'

After the supper, they left the city and went into a garden called Gethsemane. Jesus left his disciples and went a little farther into the garden. He wished to pray alone to God for strength to face the ordeal ahead.

Three times Jesus returned to find his disciples asleep. They were exhausted with grief. After a while, Judas appeared leading a troop of soldiers. Judas had arranged with the soldiers to arrest the man he would kiss, for that would be Jesus.

'Greetings, Master,' said Judas, and kissed Jesus on his cheek.

'Friend,' said Jesus, 'do what you have come to do but why must you betray me with a kiss?'

The soldiers arrested Jesus and took him to the house of the High Priest to stand trial. Peter followed the soldiers at a safe distance. He crept into the servants' hall and waited to hear news of his master.

One of the servant girls overheard Peter speak and asked him, 'Are you not one of the followers of Jesus?'

'No,' snapped Peter and joined the other servants seated by the fire. There another servant asked him, 'Have I not seen you among the disciples of Jesus?' Again Peter denied that he knew Jesus.

Finally, a third servant said, 'This man must be a friend of Jesus for he comes from Galilee.'

Terrified, Peter shouted, 'I tell you I don't know the man!' Yet before he could utter another word, the cock crowed loudly. Instantly Peter remembered the words of Jesus at supper.

Peter was overcome with grief because he knew that he had failed his master. He ran out of the house, leaving Jesus to be condemned alone, and to die at the hands of the Romans.

The stranger on the road

After Jesus had died and been buried, his followers were so miserable they did not know what to do. Either they did not fully understand, or they had forgotten all the things Jesus had told them about what would happen to him. Without their Master they were like lost sheep.

Early on the first Sunday after he had been buried, Mary Magdalene and some other women friends of Jesus went to his tomb. To their amazement, they found it was empty. Whilst they were there, some angels appeared, telling them that Jesus had already risen from the dead.

Immediately the women went and told the followers. They rushed to the tomb to see for themselves. But not all of Jesus's friends went. Two were on their way to Emmaus, a village about five miles from where they lived.

As these two walked, their minds were full of all the wonderful things Jesus had done, not only for them but for hundreds of other people. They grieved over how badly he had been treated during his last few days on earth.

With tears in their eyes they talked of how Jesus had been taken prisoner, put on trial, tortured, then crucified. Now he was dead.

After a while, the two were joined by another man walking in the same direction, who asked: 'What are you talking about so seriously, and what is making you so sad?'

Although there was something familiar about the stranger, one of the men, called Cleopus, replied, 'You must be a stranger in these parts. Do you not know what has been happening in Jerusalem these last few days?

'Surely you must have heard of Jesus of Nazareth who has worked many miracles and taught us so much about the Kingdom of God? We all hoped he would drive away the Romans and lead Israel to freedom, but our priests and rulers have crucified him.

'He died and was buried but some women we know have been to the tomb and found it empty. They told us that angels had appeared, telling them that Jesus had risen from the dead. But can such a story be true?'

'What foolish men you are,' said the stranger. 'Why are you so slow to believe what your prophets wrote many years ago? They wrote that Christ would have to suffer and die for the sins of men before he could gain the glory which God had promised him.'

Then the stranger explained more about what had been written in the scriptures. The two disciples were so interested in what the stranger told them, they begged him to stop at Emmaus and spend the evening as their guest. To this he agreed.

They took their guest to the house where they were staying and prepared a meal. All three sat down but the stranger acted as if he were the host and they were his guests.

Taking the bread in his hands, he asked God's blessing upon it. He broke the bread and handed them each a piece. The stranger did all this in exactly the same way they had seen Jesus do it many times before.

Suddenly they realized that this man was no stranger but their beloved Master, Jesus. But before they could utter a single word, he vanished.

Immediately their misery turned to joy as they said to each other, 'We should have known it was Jesus by the way he talked to us.

They were too excited to eat, and although it had been a long and tiring day, they no longer felt weary. Furthermore, it was very late but that did not bother them either. In their excitement, they hurried back to Jerusalem to tell the good news to other friends and disciples of Jesus.

Back in the capital they found their friends all awake, praying and talking about what might be happening. As Cleopus and his companion were telling their story, Jesus himself suddenly appeared in their midst and said, 'Peace be unto you.' To prove who he was, he showed them the nail marks in his hands and feet, and the wound in his side. To convince them he was not a ghost, Jesus asked them all to touch him. Then he asked for food and ate it before their eyes.

There was no longer any doubt that this was Jesus, their Master, risen from the dead, exactly as he had said he would.

More parables of Jesus

Jesus loved talking to everybody, rich and poor alike, but it was not easy for people to understand all his new teachings. For example, devout folk had been brought up to think that vengeance was a good thing. 'An eye for an eye, and a tooth for a tooth,' they believed. They found it difficult to understand Jesus when he said, 'Forgive your enemies. If a man smites you on one cheek, turn you the other also.'

So much that Jesus had to say contradicted the earlier religious teachings. Because of this Jesus often told parables, little stories which would help his listeners to understand the true meaning of what he was trying to say.

Back and forth across the land strode Jesus, followed by his faithful disciples. He preached in synagogues, on mountain-sides, in barren deserts, on sea-shores. Wherever he found people who were prepared to listen to his words, Jesus would always speak in his quiet voice, counselling wrong-doers to mend their ways, encouraging the good to help the more unfortunate.

As his fame and the stories of his amazing miracles spread across the land, so more crowds hustled to hear him speak. There are many parables that you could read, but here are three of his best-known ones.

The lost sheep

Many people could not understand why Jesus spent so much time talking to bad people and sinners. To them he said this:

'What would you think of a man who had a hundred sheep and if one went missing would not leave the other ninety-nine to go and search for the missing one? And when he found it, would he not carry it back to the flock, then call his friends and neighbours together saying, "We must celebrate the joyful news that I have found my sheep that was lost."

'In the same way there is more happiness and rejoicing in heaven over one sinner who is truly sorry and returns to God, than there is for all the good people who have no need to repent.'

The man who could not forgive

Peter asked Jesus, 'Lord, how often must I forgive my brother if he sins against me – seven times?'

'No,' said Jesus, 'seventy-seven times or as often as he says he is sorry.' Then, to explain what he meant, Jesus told the following parable:

'A king once called all his servants together to total up what he owed them or what they owed him. One servant, he discovered, owed him ten thousand pounds but had no means of paying the debt.

'The king demanded that the man, his wife and children should all be sold into slavery, and all his possessions taken and sold.

'The servant threw himself down at the king's feet, begging another chance to earn some money and pay off the debt. The king felt sorry for the man and let him off saying, "Forget about the debt."

'On his way home, this servant met a fellow servant who owed him a pound. He grabbed the poor fellow by the neck and demanded to be paid the pound that was owing to him.

'The other servant fell at his feet saying, "Please have patience and I will pay you all I owe." But the servant who was owed the money refused and had the man thrown into prison.

'This behaviour upset all the other servants who promptly told the king. The king called the man before him and said "You wicked fellow. I forgave you the debt you owed me, surely you can forgive your fellow servant."

The king was so angry, he handed the servant over to the torturers until he could repay his debt.

'My father in heaven is like the king in this story,' said Jesus, 'and will deal with all those who cannot forgive others who sin against them.'

Two houses

Some people wondered what they would learn by listening to the words of Jesus. Was it wise to follow his advice? Was he *really* the Son of God? Were the stories they had heard about his miracles true or exaggerations? To these doubters, Jesus spoke thus:

'Everyone who comes to me, and listens to my words and follows my counsel, is like a man who builds for himself a new house. He makes sure that the foundations are dug deeply and that they rest upon solid rock.

'Only then will he know that, in the time of heavy rains, when rivers rise and overflow their banks, his house will withstand the destructive floods.

'But he who listens to my words and ignores them is like a man who builds his house upon sand. When the floods come, his house will fall into ruins as he has not dug deep foundations.'

Certain people might have doubted the truth that Jesus spoke. Jesus, the Son of God, had no doubts whatsoever. Never before and never since has there been so great a man.